How Many

Rachel Gosset and Margaret Ballinger
illustrated by Karen Young

ISBN 0-590-29976-X

Published by Scholastic Inc., 555 Broadway, New York, NY 10012, by arrangement with Scholastic Australia Pty Limited.

12 11 10 9/9 0 1 2/0

Printed in the U.S.A. 08

First Scholastic printing, February 1997

SCHOLASTIC INC.
New York Toronto London Auckland Sydney

One fish in a bowl.

Two fish in a pond.

Three fish in a stream.

Four fish in a lake.

Five fish in a river.

Six fish in the sea.